The Circle of Life:

It Begins with Z and Ends with A

TIJAN BROWN

Balboa Press books may be ordered through booksellers or by contacting:

Balboa Press
A Division of Hay House
1663 Liberty Drive
Bloomington, IN 47403
www.balboapress.com
844-682-1282

Because of the dynamic nature of the Internet, any web addresses or links contained in this book may have changed since publication and may no longer be valid. The views expressed in this work are solely those of the author and do not necessarily reflect the views of the publisher, and the publisher hereby disclaims any responsibility for them.

Any people depicted in stock imagery provided by Getty Images are models, and such images are being used for illustrative purposes only.
Certain stock imagery © Getty Images.

ISBN: 978-1-5043-5010-5 (sc)
ISBN: 978-1-5043-5011-2 (e)

Library of Congress Control Number: 2016901607

Print information available on the last page.

Balboa Press rev. date: 11/16/2021

I have always been curious about the details of life, how we are related beyond what we see to each other and to the world in which we live. It is my great hope to awaken each reader to set upon a personal journey with the purpose of understanding the relationship between the food we eat, its life force energy, and the effects on the body.

We have been given everything we need to support human existence by Mother Earth.

I dedicate this offering to the world and to the community with whom it is shared. May we learn to take care of the planet and each other and self.

In community, Tijan Brown

Z = Zapote & Zygote

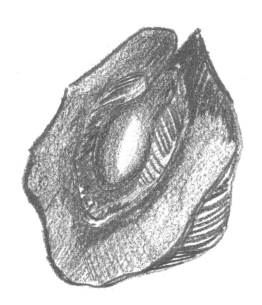

Zapote is indigenous to the hills of Peru. Full of antibacterial, antiviral and anti-parasitic antioxidants, benefits of the zapote fruit include a high volume of dietary fiber, vitamins A and C, as well as other nutrients that are part of a healthy body.

A zygote is the result of a synthesized union of two gametes, which results in the form of a human being.

Y = Yucca & Yellow Marrow

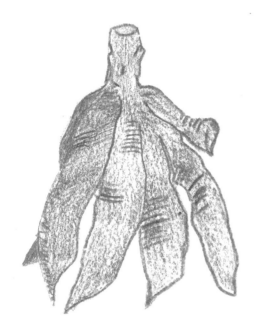

Yucca root contains an active compound called steroidal saponin. This compound has been shown to reduce the stiffness, pain and swelling associated with conditions of the skeletal system such as bursitis, gout, arthritis and rheumatism.

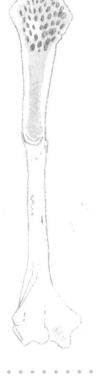

Yellow marrow is a tissue of the skeletal system which stores lipids as energy reserves for bone tissue found at the ends of long bones.

X = Xigua & Water

Xigua fruit, also known as watermelon is 92% water, making the xigua fruit an eXcellent source of water.

One of the benefits of water is that it carries nutrients and oxygen to cells. Water also supports the lymphatic system, urinary system and the digestive system by carrying waste out of the body through lymph, pee and doodoo.

W = Watercress & Waste

Watercress is one of many vegetables that support a healthy lymphatic system.

Located in strategic parts of the body, lymph nodes help to remove waste products and debris from tissues. Lymph nodes resemble a bushel of watercress.

V = Vitamins & Various bodily functions

There are 4 fat-soluble vitamins (A, D, E, and K) and 9 water-soluble vitamins (C, B1-Thiamine, B2-Riboflavin, B3-Niacin, B5-Pantothenic acid, B6-Pyridoxine, B7-Biotin, B9-Folic Acid, and B12-Cyanocobalamin).

Understanding the nutritional value of food contributes to a healthier life. For example, fat-soluble foods keep the body functioning at optimum levels by keeping bones strong, protecting the body from free radicals, and they keep eyes healthy. Fat-soluble foods include: fish, meat, eggs, green leafy vegetables, and carrots.

Water-soluble foods keep the body functioning at optimum levels by changing carbohydrates in food to energy, assisting the breakdown of fats and forming collagen, which is an important protein of skin tissue and joints. Water-soluble foods include: fruits, vegetables, grains, and dairy.

U = Ugli fruit & Uvula

The Ugli fruit is a cross between a grapefruit, a tangerine, and an orange.

Ugli fruit is high in vitamin C which helps keep your immune system strong, which in turn can prevent a swollen uvula that could be the result of a bacterial or viral infection.

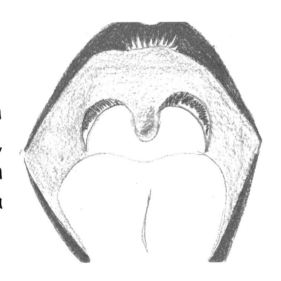

T = Tomato & Temporal lobe

The shape of the tomato closely resembles the human brain. Sliced in half, the quadrants of the tomato resemble the four main lobes of the human brain.

The four main lobes of the brain include temporal, frontal, parietal, and occipital. Tomatoes are rich in antioxidants that support brain function.

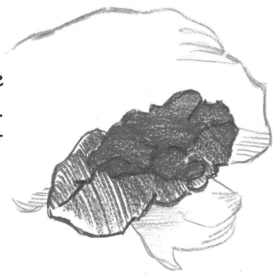

S = Sweet Potatoes & Pancreas

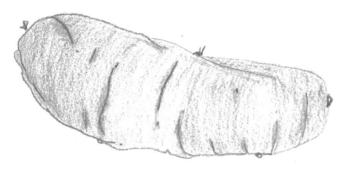

Sweet Potatoes look like your pancreas. Sweet Potatoes are a good source of fiber, vitamin A, vitamin C and vitamin B6.

They can help stabilize blood sugar levels and lower insulin resistance. Sweet potatoes are high in fiber and have a low glycemic index; which means they will have less effect on blood sugar and insulin levels.

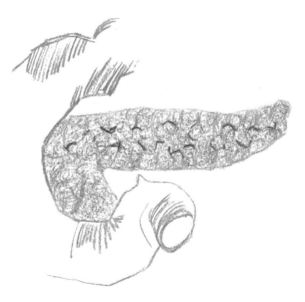

R = Red Bell Pepper & Red Blood Cells

Red Bell Peppers are considered extremely nutrient dense and benefit the body in a number of ways, specifically bone health. Red bell peppers look like red blood cells, which the body produces in bone marrow.

Red blood cells produced in the bone marrow serve an important role of carrying oxygen from the lungs to the rest of the body.

Q = Quandong & Quadricep muscles

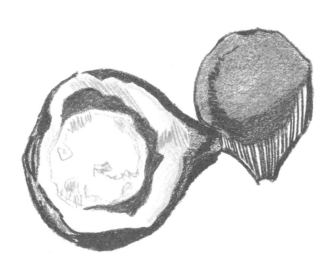

Quandong is a fruit indigenous to the arid regions of Australia. And is a wonderful source of Vitamin E, folate, magnesium and calcium. A rich source of phenolic-based

antioxidants which reduces inflammation protecting against a number of diseases.

The quandong fruit has also been found to have high levels of Vitamin C, which helps to support the muscular system of the body supporting quicker recovery after a workout. The quadriceps muscle group is the largest muscle grouping in the body.

P = Papaya & Prostate Gland

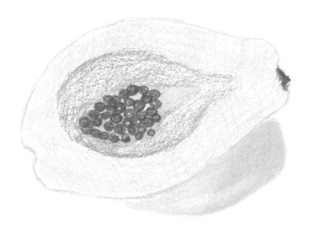

Papaya fruit is a source of dietary fiber, Vitamins A, C and E as well as folate and antioxidants. Like many tropical fruits, the papaya fruit is rich in antioxidants that fight against free radicals in the body.

Papaya looks like the prostate gland which is part of the male anatomy and is located just below the bladder.

They are known to be a powerful antioxidant, containing lycopene and are good options to boost prostate health.

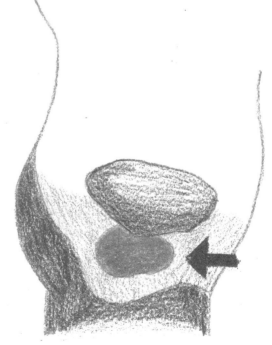

O = Onions & Oligodendrocytes

Layers of an onion, when compared with oligodendrocytes under a microscope, show similarities in their branchlike shape.

While onions help to move waste materials from cells, oligodendrocytes provide support to nerve cells in the central nervous system by enabling fast saltatory conduction that moves electrical impulses from node to node down the full length of an axon.

N = Nuts & Neurons

Nuts can enhance neurological functions by helping to control stress while neurons transmit information through electrical and chemical signals. Nuts help to slow down the brains aging process as well as increase memory.

The Cashew is a great example of how a nut mirrors a body part. The shape of the cashew nut is like the shape of the hippocampus; the hippocampus directly affects short-term memory.

M = Mango & Meninges

The meninges' serve to protect the central nervous system of the brain which is tucked away nicely in the center of the skull.

Like the meninges, the mango fruit containing tartaric acid and malic acid that support the alkali reserve of the body also protect the seed tucked away nicely in the center of this heavenly fruit.

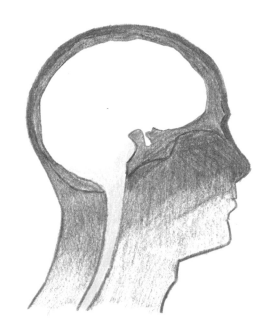

L = Lemons & Lactiferous ducts

Similar in shape to a breast, the lemon fruit contains hundreds of lobules that carry the liquid of the fruit.

Lactiferous ducts form a tree branched system connecting the lobules of the mammary gland, that are like the tree branched system that connect the lobules of the lemon fruit.

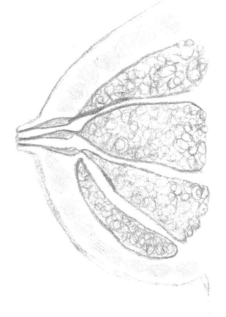

K = Kidney Beans & Kidneys

Kidney beans look very much like a kidney organ, the human organs that support the urinary system. The kidneys also regulate electrolytes, maintenance of acid-base balance and blood pressure.

Kidney beans contain manganese which is an important mineral supporting the breakdown of free radicals of the mitochondria in the kidneys. Mitochondria help maintain cellular balance of this organ and others.

J = Jujube & Jejunum

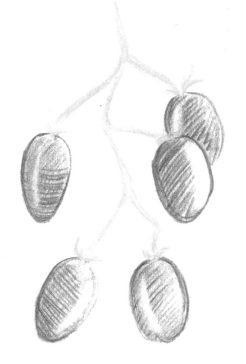

Health properties of the jujube fruit include: antifungal, antibacterial, antiulcer, have anti-inflammatory properties and are rich in antioxidants.

Sweet tasting fresh jujubes support and look like the jejunum, the second portion of the small intestine.

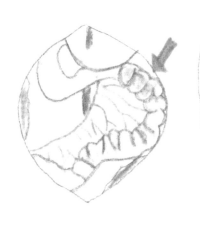

I = Ita Palm Fruit & Intestinal Villus

Properties of the ita palm fruit contribute to the health and balance of the intestinal tract helping to fight against illness and disease.

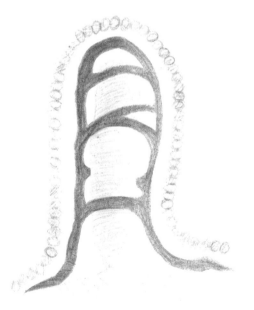

Intestinal villi are small, leaf-like projections that fan out from the lining of the intestinal wall; like the leaves of the ita palm tree that fan out from the trunk.

H = Honeydew Melon & Dermis

One way to support the dermis, the inner layer of the two main layers of the skin, is by consuming honeydew melon.

Honeydew melon has a unique property when perfectly ripe will not wrinkle on the skin's surface. Eating honeydew melon may support healthy skin due to high vitamin C content. Vitamin C is essential for the proper production of collagen, a key component for repairing and maintaining skin tissue.

G = Grapefruit & Mammary Glands

The grapefruit when cut in half looks like the mammary gland of the female and assist the health of breasts and the movement of lymph in and out of the breasts.

Grapefruit contains limonoids, phytochemicals found in sweet or sour-scented citrus fruits and other plants, and is a substance known to inhibit the growth of tumors.

F = Fennel bulb & Flatulence

The fennel bulb with is round form, looks like a bloated stomach. A bloated stomach happens when gas builds up in the digestive tract when undigested food gets broken down or when you swallow air.

Fennel bulb contains aspartic acid that can be used by infants and the elderly to expel gas from the stomach and soothing swelling or irritation in the intestines and improve digestion.

E = Eggplant & Epidermis

Eggplants are rich in Vitamin C, which protects your skin and body from oxidative damage as well as other signs of aging, including fine lines and wrinkles.

As an anti-aging agent, eggplants have been used in parts of Asia, the Middle East, and Turkey to pamper skin and have even been used to fade sun spots.

D = Dates & Doo-Doo

Dates are a delicious fruit which can be enjoyed fresh or dried. Dates support a healthy digestive tract by being one of natures' natural laxatives. Dried dates are a sweet and delicious snack that can be consumed as an alternative to chocolate, cookies and other sugary processed treats.

C = Carrots & Cornea

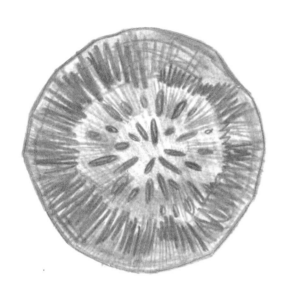

A slice of carrot looks like the cornea. A carrot is a dicot root that forms successive cambia, and multiple rings of vascular bundles that radiate out towards the outer edges. The cornea is the clear outer layer at the front of the eye, that helps your eye to focus light so you can see clearly.

Carrots are a good source of beta carotene that the body converts into Vitamin A, a nutrient that helps you see in the dark. Carrots are also a

good source of lutein, which benefit eye health and protect against age-related degenerative eye diseases.

B = Banana & Back

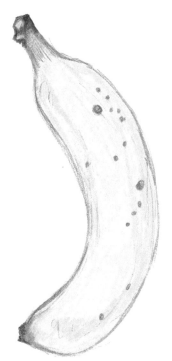

A banana has the same shape as the three main curves of the back: cervical, thoracic and the lumbar which make up the spinal column.

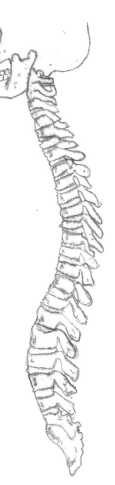

The nutrients in bananas help support many of the body's functions; one being the support of calcium absorption for strong bones.

A = Avocado & A womb

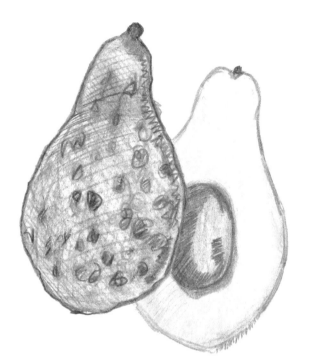

An avocado has the same shape as a womb. The avocado has been found to target the health and the function of the womb and cervix during pregnancy.

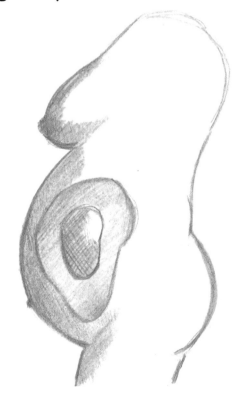

An avocado can take up to 8 or 9 months from flower to harvest. Roughly the same gestational period of a full term human after the synthesized union of two gametes, which form the zygote.

Thank you for sharing the journey. Through the creative process of writing and drawing, I've deepened my understanding of our human connection to the planet...and it is my hope that the same occurs with you.

Allow mindfulness and kindness to guide you on your journey of discovery, keeping the body and planet healthy and vital.

Special thanks to Marie Whitman, of EatYourPoem.com, for her critical eye and creative spirit; Tiffany Totah, for her unconditional love and support; Patrick 'Chance' Fulerton, for his creative support; and Eric Gordon, of DCCreepers. blogspot.com, for his creative support and attention to details.

My parents and step-parent who have always encouraged my creative spirit. And to my loving husband – thank you for being the man who makes "good life decisions".

Printed in the United States
by Baker & Taylor Publisher Services